Praise for the first U.S. Edition of
A Flight Attendant's FULL DISCLOSURE

"Becky Woodbridge is a dynamic, innovative leader and speaker. It's not surprising that her first book is a captivating and informative read that has what it takes to help people transform their business and personal relationships."

–**David J. Pollay**, Founder of PollayCoaching.com and bestselling author of *The Law of the Garbage Truck*®

"The term 'customer service' has become a cliché in global business. Too many shrug it off, yet the implications of poor customer service for a flight crew can have dire consequences. She provides clear advice on how to take strategies from 30,000 feet and apply them at ground level in your business and life. The book drives home the point that customer service isn't a nice-to-have in business, it IS the business."

–**Mace Horoff**, Medical Sales/High-Stakes Sales Expert and author of *Mastering Medical Sales* and *The Sex in Sales: Dirty Little Secrets of Sales Success.*

"Becky shows rock solid accuracy with her stories about life in the skies. She has a colorful knack for describing the good, the bad, the ugly, and the wondrous, and she quickly had my memories flooding back. Her long career, though we never crossed paths, parallels mine in so many ways. Her supportive ideas turn the book into a wonderful manual for integrity and common courtesy in business and everywhere else.

–**Sharon Eldred**, Retired 30-year flight attendant for another major airline

"This is a powerful book that translates real stories, along with humorous airline metaphors, into a success-driven primer for any business large or small. It's an educational eye-opener as to why customer service is tantamount to any organization."

–**David Mezzapelle**, bestselling author of the *Contagious Optimism* book series

"Becky Woodbridge, professional speaker and executive coach, brilliantly weaves lessons learned from years of experience as a flight attendant and lands them directly into the heart of business. Her witty and authentic style had me laughing out loud as the comparisons ring true to what we have all experienced as both business owners and customers. She offers practical ways to integrate her ideas into immediately executable actions that can immediately impact customer service."

–**Laurie Riquelmy**, Executive Coach

"I was truly amazed at the number of confounding dilemmas Becky experiences while in the sky. Ms. Woodbridge does a great job at articulating the parallels between what flight crews deal with and real-world business situations. The true stories came to life as I read them, causing me to pause and reflect on my own past behaviors. In the end, it's all about providing a great customer experience. Wonderful book for anyone to take to heart and to work."

–**Erik Mintz**, CEO, DealCoachPro

A FLIGHT ATTENDANT'S
FULL DISCLOSURE

How to Manage

Customer Service Breakdowns

BECKY WOODBRIDGE

SKYWITCH

PUBLISHING

SKYWITCH

PUBLISHING

P.O.1605
Durango, Colorado 81302
U.S.A.

Skywitch™ Publishing and the Skywitch logo are trademarks of
SkyBitch™ LLC (USA)
LIBRARY OF CONGRESS
CATALOGING -IN-PUBLICATION DATA
has been applied for.

ISBN: 978-0-9993304-0-1

Cover design and interior artwork by National Impressions
Cover photo by VMA Studios
Edited by Brenda Robinson, PotentPen.com
Dennis Miller quote used by permission

DEDICATION

This book is dedicated to Mom; Dad; sisters Kelly, Velinda, Kim, and Sherry; brother Greg (who's like a sister); and, last but not least, my beautiful daughter EJ. My heart is full of love for my family.

"Sheriff" Becky (Center rear) and Siblings

Mom & Dad

EJ

CONTENTS

ACKNOWLEDGMENTS

This book would not have been possible without so many people cheering me on. The support of my family and friends is beyond measure. They put up with my ongoing storytelling of my adventures and airline stories until I'm sure they are fogged over. I will always be grateful to my dear friend, the talented writer Kevin Kaminski. Kevin's ability to listen well and his continuing patience to get the stories to review and rewrite will always hold a special place in my heart.

 Gavin and Mandy Robin of Damn Good Agency, who always saw my potential in any crazy idea I had and, for whatever reason, will take a call from me at any time of day or night, always willing to listen and encourage me to go big. I could not build a brand without their damn good agency— and I mean damn good.

My absolute favorite coach and friend of all time, Laurie Riquelmy, former owner of Education for Living Seminars (EFL), is directly responsible for my growth as a human being so that I am a better person, family member, friend and customer service professional. I am thankful for Chuck Smith, founder of EFL, whose passion for change, his wisdom, and his masterful way of coaching also paved the way for me to do what I do today. Without its coaches, (EFL is now owned by Stephanie and Jill Chandler-Simpson) I would not have been able to recognize the impact I make on the world.

I'm also deeply grateful to Julio Olalla, Newfield Network founder and master ontological coach, who taught me about the world of coaching, inspiring me to go out into the world with more to offer than I could have ever imagined, and for his wisdom in knowing that I needed to go slow to go far. To my friends Celia and Bill Finnen, Mahi and Rick Wing and Karen Marando. They have always been right there beside me making sure I'm proceeding in a forward motion, keeping my wackiness in moderation, and watching over my path to success. They all have the most amazing energy that supports and nourishes me when times get tough.

For Meredith Eicher and her dad, John Eicher, for a hand up when I was out of hands, and for always believing in me. Special thanks to my friend Deanne Prymek for being my mirror when I'm having a breakdown, who never backs down from her authentic self, who is a fierce woman's advocate and truly a powerful coach. For Nicole Valentino for showing up at my door with boxes and chocolate cake when I needed a friend at that most appropriate moment of time. For John and Tony Whittner, who took me under their wings like I've known them my entire life, and who help me be accountable.

TO ALL FLIGHT ATTENDANTS

Leaving your home is never easy for anyone. Traveling is unpredictable and exhausting to say the least. From dealing with traffic, parking, security and the mile or two you have to walk to get to your gate is no easy feat, but to do this grind every time you go to work can make anyone bonkers before you even start your work day. Not to mention that entire part I just spoke about is unpaid! For flight attendants, the time clock doesn't begin to calculate their pay until the airplane pushes back from the gate. So, all those boarding issues and delays and the stress to get the plane off on time is a freebie from the flight crews. And don't forget the stress of wondering if there is going to be another threat to the airplane.

A flight attendant's job is many things. They deal with new customers every day from cross cultures, everyone with their own mood and way of being so that each flight is a completely different complexity to deal with— not to mention they are away from their families. Flight attendants are some of the warmest, friendliest, compassionate people I know. They have incredible patience and wisdom to help out in any situation, but like most human beings, they have their fair share of personal breakdowns that get in the way when dealing with the traveling public. So, I say hats off to the flight attendants who go to work in the most unusual environment and create a nice place for everyone to be until they get you to your destination in a safe and timely manner. Thank you to the thousands of flight attendants with whom I've shared many great moments. Through our laughter and tears, my fellow flight attendants will always be a part of my core. From jump seat therapy, to wild and crazy layovers, through long delays and misconnects, and just plain weird and nutty flights.

And lastly, I thank the recruiter who had the wherewithal to hire me thirty years ago among thousands of women. I've been given the most incredible thirty years as a flight attendant traveling the world.

FOREWORD

"We will be landing shortly, so please bring your seat backs to their full upright and locked position."

That's what the in-flight announcement said. But, full disclosure, what did it mean?

Possible passenger reaction: Aren't we going to use the full landing strip instead of landing "short-ly"? If not, why not?

The common practice of saying "shortly" when you mean "soon" originated in the Southern USA where that is the colloquial meaning. "See you shortly," means I will see you soon. But to most people short means short and "short" is not full length. That's just one little benign example of how our ways of communicating can often work against our efforts to get through to others.

In *Full Disclosure*, Becky Woodbridge tells the insider's stories of what flight attendants see and do, plus she tells you how they feel. You'll hear some stories that sound like your own, and some that are far outside of your personal experiences. More importantly, you will learn how to make difficult situations better and how to get results with even the most challenging people.

Becky's years of flight service all over the world in both good and awful circumstances have enabled her to understand and deal with some of the toughest interpersonal conflicts. She will show you the thinking behind the behaviors, and the best ways to diffuse conflict and show compassion.

As I learned from Becky, I also gained a great respect for her integrity and character. She genuinely cares about helping others. It shows in the ways that she shares her own foibles and admits the times she's been ashamed of her own actions. This book will support you in becoming more of the good person we all hope to be, and in knowing how to deal with the worst of situations. Once you've read it, pass it around, leave one in the seat back pocket for the next passenger, and buy a copy for everyone in your organization. The ensuing discussions will cause you to retain more customers and improve both performance and retention among employees.

In the Spirit of Service,
Jim Cathcart, CSP, CPAE
Author of *Relationship Selling* and founder of Cathcart.com
Thousand Oaks, California

INTRODUCTION

"There's no reason to become alarmed, and we hope you'll enjoy the rest of your flight. By the way, is there anyone on board who knows how to fly a plane?"

—Flight attendant Elaine Dickinson (Julie Hagerty), in the movie "Airplane!"

I've been employed as a flight attendant on the same major airline for more than thirty years. Not once during that time have I pulled an Elaine Dickinson in mid-flight. Nor have I ever placed a baby in an overhead bin. Or accidentally packed a loaded handgun in my carry-on bag. And, no, I wasn't the one who asked Alec Baldwin to stop playing "Words with Friends" on his mobile phone. (The latter three incidents, by the way, all really happened to other flight attendants.)

But, in the spirit of full disclosure, I have seen my share of cabin pressure over the years. Strange things tend to happen when you're hurtling through thin air at six- hundred mph in an enclosed tube. Restlessness sets in. Emotions begin to fray. Patience wears thin. Tempers flare.

And that's just among the crew. Listen, there's a reason why it takes one hundred flight attendants to change a light bulb. One has to change it... and ninety- nine have to bitch about it.

That's an old stereotype, but punch lines can carry a little nugget of truth. And the truth about air travel is this: According to the United States Department of Transportation's Bureau of Transportation Statistics (BTS), 932.0 million systemwide (domestic and international) (and on foreign airlines that serve this country) scheduled passengers traveled in 2016. That breaks down to roughly ten million domestic and international flights.

Think about it. More passengers stepped aboard a domestic airline (or a plane that serves the U.S.) than the combined populations of Italy, Germany, France, Russia, Spain, Turkey, Japan and the United Kingdom. That's a lot of people returning their seats to an upright position in the course of one calendar year.

Considering that the average passenger trip in 2011 (again, according to BTS) covered 1,474.6 miles, it's also ample opportunity for someone in my profession to observe the human condition— in rather close quarters.

I've been interacting with passengers on domestic and international flights since May 1987. You name the plane—MD-80, DC-10, Boeing 747, Boeing 777, Airbus A300—and I'm qualified to work inside of it. In addition to being based in New York, Chicago, Boston, Miami and Los Angeles, I've flown to 48 of the 50 states (North Dakota and South Dakota, you're on my bucket list!).

For all but one of my years as a flight attendant, I've been the purser. That required additional training at the beginning of my career—and resulted in more pay—but it also meant more responsibility. I'm the person who serves as a liaison between my team and the cockpit crew, and who oversees all in-flight service procedures and who handles passenger concerns.

Most importantly, when lines of communication collapse between passenger and flight attendant, between passenger and passenger, between two or more flight attendants, between flight attendant and pilot, I'm often the person who has to figure out how to reconnect them.

Communication breakdown in everyday life is a challenge, but at 30,000 feet the stakes can be even higher (pardon the pun). One wrong word, and what started as a small complaint in seat 12A can turn into a flight-long battle that unnerves passengers in rows 10 to 20. One inaccurate assessment of a situation, and the woman with a serious fear of flying in first class can send all of coach into a panic.

Of course, not every flight produces an uncomfortable confrontation. Sometimes, passenger concerns consist of nothing more than a bag that won't fit in an overhead compartment, a lack of blankets on a long flight, a child throwing peanuts across the aisle, or a waiting line for the back bathroom because some couple is trying to join the "Mile High Club."

I've seen a little bit of everything in my 30 years of flying the friendly (and sometimes not-so-friendly) skies—and you'll read many of those stories in the ensuing pages. But it wasn't until the past decade that I really started to appreciate how the lessons I was learning at altitude could successfully translate to the business world.

I know what you're thinking. What does dealing with the passenger who inhaled eight mini-bottles of Jim Beam have to do with the employees at my small start-up business or the team I oversee at a Fortune 500 company?

If we're talking about the subsequent need for an airsickness bag after mini- bottle number 12, not much. But if we're talking about how to better understand your customer, how to communicate more effectively, and how to implement strategies that not only solve immediate problems but that have long-term impact... well, then dealing with Mr. Jim Beam may just resonate.

In fact, I've seen it resonate. Over and over again.

For several years, in addition to my career with the airline, I ran my own highly-rated real estate company in South Florida. The two work environments couldn't have been more different on paper—but a common thread quickly emerged, one that led me to my current role as a professional speaker with programs to serve businesses throughout the Southeast.

Communication may be a two-way street, but it only takes one voice to set the tone. Not only have I learned this the hard way in dealings with flight teams and passengers, but I also witnessed it firsthand from the perspective of a businesswoman and a coach. Throughout the pages of this book, we'll discuss the many ways our interactions with one another impact us professionally and personally.

And then we'll set about easing that cabin pressure—and realizing our potential—by strengthening communication, enhancing employer/employee relations, creating a more productive work atmosphere and improving customer relationships. We'll address a variety of customer-service challenges based on my years as a flight attendant. We'll discuss everything from identifying and dealing with different moods in the workplace to viewing customers and co-workers without judgment, to diffusing contentious situations.

So please fasten your seatbelt! We're about to take off!

Becky Woodbridge

December 2017

1: IT'S NOT THE CHICKEN

Back when airlines still served meals in coach class (remember those days?), passengers often had a choice between chicken and beef. It truly wasn't quite as appealing or palatable to hungry passengers as a delicious serving of lobster Newburg, but it sure beat a bag of peanuts.

One time, a flight attendant pulled me aside and explained that a passenger in her section was losing it because he didn't get his chicken. As the purser on this particular flight, it was my job to handle customer complaints. Not only was I new at the position, but also the airline didn't give us direct training in communication breakdowns. Our training was how to serve you Coke and pretzels.

So, I went to the back of the plane thinking the worst. I had neither the experience nor the tools to handle a heated confrontation. So instead of formulating a strategy for dealing with the situation, I thought to myself, "What a spoiled brat. We don't have chicken. Big deal. I can't pull a chicken out of my ass. Eat, or don't eat. Either way, get over it."

Of course, I didn't actually say this. But, trust me, I wanted to.

Instead, I explained—with little-to-no empathy in my voice—that we receive x-number of chicken dinners per flight. Unfortunately, more people had ordered chicken than beef, and we had run out. In truth, more people always ordered chicken. The airline should have had enough chicken to cover the requests. It didn't.

The passenger, as my fellow flight attendant had warned me, did not take the news well.

"You've got to be kidding me," he said "That man has chicken. That lady has chicken. That kid has chicken. Why can't I get my damned chicken? This is bull."

It took me several more years to understand that the passenger's reaction had little to do with chicken. Or that my reaction—doing next to nothing to actually appease the man and soothe the situation—compounded the mistake by making the passenger feel even worse about the airline.

The customer isn't always right. But today, unlike that episode, I believe in making them right.

Let's say a customer walks into your hardware store with a defective drill bit that he purchased a few days earlier. The customer is none too pleased—and the drill bit is the least of it. His wife is nagging him at home. His son is whining. He just received a pay cut at work. And his favorite football team just lost.

He desperately needs this drill bit—but he's about to unleash some serious frustration that runs far deeper than inadequate hardware.

As a business owner, do you fear this scenario? Or is this an opportunity?

Trust me, it's a window. And it's a really big one. It's your moment to make the situation right. Take advantage of it. Change this customer's story. Fulfill his expectations and solve the problem—and then take it one step further. Give that customer a reason to return..

The opportunity is there to create a customer for life!

If three decades of flying the sometimes not-so-friendly skies has taught me anything, it's that passengers want this kind of validation. They crave it.

Do you really think a passenger loses sleep over an airline's chicken policy? In reality, it's everything that has led up to that particular moment—especially in our country's post-9/11 world—that causes the chicken meltdown.

It's paying baggage fees that used to be part of the ticket. It's having to arrive two hours before your flight—and still barely boarding in time because the security line is so long. It's having security remove your shampoo and mouthwash because you forgot to put them in three-ounce containers. It's having to take off your belt, your shoes, your jewelry— and still being asked to step inside that strange full-body X- ray scanner. It's being asked ridiculous questions, like if your bags have been in your possession the whole time.

No wonder passengers are upset the minute they board. No wonder something like chicken, or lack thereof, can cause someone to blow a gasket. The chicken is big. It stands for something. People aren't getting what they feel like they deserve when it comes to air travel. They feel rushed, abused, slighted, and deprived. Their experience has been diminished so much that they walk into the airport with more dread than anticipation.

As a flight attendant, I'm dealing with more than two hundred such passengers in a confined tube on a given trip. Now, multiply that by the two thousand seven hundred flights per day flown by major airlines. And then stretch that out over three hundred and sixty-five days.

How can you possibly keep that many people happy—people already bearing the scars of past dealings with airlines? You can't. Not all of them.

You can, however, make a difference. One customer at a time.

Our passenger is the throes of an adult tantrum. He paid good money for his flight, probably too much in his estimation. He's hungry, and now he's over-the-moon ticked-off because we can't provide the chicken on this flight!

Now what?

Had I known then what I know now, I would have taken a much more direct and sympathetic approach. For starters, I would have acknowledged the obvious.

"I'm so sorry. Unfortunately, the airline did not estimate nearly enough chicken, especially given all the passengers who prefer chicken. You're the unfortunate one who didn't get what he asked for.

"You're right. We made a mistake."

Admit the error; confession, after all, is good for the soul. Call out the elephant in the room. You've already broken the bond of trust. Don't compound that mistake by dancing around the truth.

Businesses sometimes fail by making excuses instead of immediately apologizing. Every business is going to make mistakes. And human beings, by our very nature, want to defend those mistakes. We want to tell you why we screwed up in hope that you'll somehow see our side of the story.

All that does is make the customer feel worse. They don't want to hear excuses; they want an acceptance that you made a mistake—and that you'll do everything in your power to fix it.

So, give that to them.

Make the customer right. That's what the customer wants. Validate them, and you'll help them feel valued and appreciated.

I eventually learned my lesson. In later years, when we ran out of a dish or, in the post-chicken/beef era, when a passenger was hungry, I would do anything I could to secure food. I'd look for an extra meal in first class. I'd try and sweet-talk one of the pilots out of his dinner. I'd even offer passengers food that I had brought on board.

One time, during a layover in Louisiana, a good friend of mine cooked me some tasty Cajun-flavored pasta with crawfish. I packed the leftovers and put them in the airplane refrigerator, fully intending to relive that meal during a break. I ended up giving it to a starving passenger. It's not often that a person will take food from a stranger. But on a plane, just as in business, customers always will gratefully accept an act of kindness from someone caring.

2: HOW MOODS CAN CLIP YOUR WINGS

One flight attendant to another: *"You don't count my ex-husbands and I won't count your calories."*

Flight attendants see everything. Don't think for a moment that you're pulling one over on us. We've seen and heard it all. We know what's going on underneath the blanket not-so-discreetly positioned over the laps of passengers in seats 24A and 24B. We see the "hidden" flask of alcohol that you're pouring into your Diet Coke. And we know that your girlfriend isn't joining you in the bathroom on the overnight flight because she's worried you're not feeling well.

On the other hand, flight attendants need to understand that passengers see and hear as well. We're not invisible just because we're standing in the galley and out of sight from the people in the first few rows.

Case in point.

I was with a Los Angeles-based crew working a short flight from Austin to Dallas, about thirty minutes in the air. Another flight attendant was catching a ride back to her home base in Dallas after a long shift, but she was out of uniform. Still, everyone sitting in first class knew she was a flight attendant because she was sitting in the jump seat.

Oh yes, she also had been drinking—which is illegal, even for an off-duty airline employee in the jump seat.

After the safety demo, a few of the flight attendants were chatting with their off-duty co-worker. The chat quickly turned into one-woman bitch session—and, fueled by her pre-flight cocktails, it was getting louder by the second.

"This f------ airline and its cuts," she bitched. "What a joke. I want my goddamn vacation days back."

I had to walk up to the jump seat and literally shush her up, like I was talking to a four-year-old.

About twenty minutes later, the captain was telling us to prepare for landing. As the working attendants were tending to passengers, our intoxicated guest left her jump seat and commandeered the PA system.

"The only reason you people were served drinks today is that this L.A.-based crew is one of the best in the business," she said in a voice that left no doubt that she was still feeling the effects of her cocktails. "Had this been a Dallas crew, trust me, you wouldn't have gotten drinks."

A week later, I received a note from my supervisor. One of the passengers in first class that day was a Dallas businessman, and he was none too pleased that our drunk friend had trashed his hometown. After all, you don't mess with Texas.

Moreover, this businessman had heard every derogatory comment the off-duty attendant had made about the airline—and he was in the last row of first class. That means every single person in first class heard her rant.

"When you have employees that disgruntled, it truly worries me," the businessman wrote in a letter to the supervisor. "I can't trust a company whose employees display that kind of contempt. So, I will no longer be flying on your airline."

Part of the reason I enjoy speaking to businesses is because I've been in the trenches. I understand and appreciate the value of continuing education—whether it's training connected to a new technology or a simple reminder of the pillars of strong customer service. I wish that, over the years, my airline had paid more attention to that part of its business. We certainly could have used it.

Now that I am a part of the speaking industry, I see, up close, the impact that a simple yearly seminar can have when it comes to keeping employees engaged. I've listened to experts wow an audience with news of cutting-edge advancements. I've seen entrepreneurs speak to the spirit of possibility. And I've watched standout business speakers inspire crowds by addressing any number of big-picture topics—from accountability and excellence in leadership to communication and increased productivity.

But there's one topic that rarely, if ever, receives its due when it comes to the success or failure of a business.

Moods.

Moods drive us. Moods come in the door before we do. Think about a typical morning at your place of work. There's John, he's always on edge early in the day because of his long drive in rush-hour traffic. There's Melissa, she brings morning treats for the staff and couldn't be more pleasant. There's Zach, he's in the zone and ready to conquer the world. And there's Suzette, who never seems to have anything nice to say about anyone.

Everyone comes to work with a mood. And those moods, if not acknowledged and understood, can be the difference between a high-flying company and one that's grounded and in need of repairs.

I wake up every morning peppy, upbeat, optimistic and ready to go. Recently, I was living with a friend of mine, someone who was not a morning person. She needed a good thirty minutes to have her coffee and ease into the day; she didn't want to talk, beyond a quick morning hello.

This could have been a source of immediate conflict between us. Instead, I learned to recognize her mood and adjust accordingly.

That's just interaction between two individuals. Multiply that by the number of people in your business, and think about how such a tangled web might impact company culture.

Now, consider this: It only takes one mood—one unchecked, unacknowledged mood—to create a major problem. The drunk, disgruntled flight attendant who overheard bad mouthing the company? She cost the airline at least one paying customer—and probably, through word of mouth, other potential fares. Major airlines schedule as many as seven thousand flights per day. Imagine what losing just one customer every ten flights could cost an airline in actual dollars.

In this case, human error was the culprit. The flight attendant's resentment had damaged the trust that the airline had built up with that customer.

Resentment is one of four common moods. There is resentment and resignation, which go hand in hand. And there's peace and ambition, which also go together. Clearly, a company wants its employees in the latter category, but as we all know, it's not that simple.

An airline has an identity that comes from the mood of its employees. When I first started as a flight attendant, the mood was generally upbeat. Attendants, especially, felt more recognized for their contributions. We were taken much more seriously as employees, especially compared to the Sexy Seventies—the days of stewardesses clad in go-go boots and slogans like, "Come Fly Me!"

But over time, resentments began to build. Airlines began making significant cuts. Longtime employees were shown the door. Benefits were diminished. Bonuses were slashed or eliminated altogether—except at the highest levels. Not only did employees feel undervalued, they felt lied to.

Soon, that mood begins to trickle down, permeating everything involving employees. They say that when the plane's engines shut off, there is still whining going on. That's the flight attendants.

Once, after a flight landed, I remember telling the next crew boarding the plane that we were missing six wheelchairs. "Well, when they outsource us, this is going to happen," one of the agents said. "If they cut me from working here, I'm going to sit back and watch them suffer."

You think moods can't affect the bottom line? Think again. Once loyalty and trust go out the window, all bets are off.

Resentful employees don't have your back. Any company with that problem is in trouble.

By the way, not all resentment is so passive.

More and more, I see people refusing to do anything that might benefit the company. Instead, they worry only about themselves. Or, worse yet, they look to get even (a classic offshoot of resentment). I've seen flight attendants throw away perfectly good food/beverage products, steal things, and even purposely try to delay flights. When you're concentrating on getting even, you're not concentrating on your job.

But the trickle-down effect doesn't end there. The man who wrote my supervisor a letter was right. Disgruntled employees are eventually going to do something that's not in the best interest of the customer.

Suddenly, you have a lot of ticked off people. Passengers are mad because they feel their own experience has been diminished. Airline employees are mad because the industry they grew up loving no longer exists. And we're all hurtling through the air in this enclosed tube at 35,000 feet. Too many moods to count. Too much resentment to bear.

If peace and ambition are our destinations, how can we possibly get there when resentment and resignation have hijacked the plane?

Simple. One customer at a time.

One time, a new flight attendant overcooked the meal of a first-class passenger. The man stormed up to the galley and said in a clearly agitated voice, "Who's in charge?"

"I am," I responded.

"This meal is unacceptable," he said.

"Would you prefer to have the beef?" I asked.

"Prefer." That was the word that set him off. No, he did not "prefer" beef. He preferred what he had, the chicken. It just wasn't prepared to his satisfaction. He literally started screaming at me in the galley. "I paid good money to be in this section! And this is the service I get? Are you kidding me?"

Now, I was livid. And my inexperience as a customer service person showed. I told him he better calm down or I was going to have him tossed off the plane.

There's no way to predict which word or phrase will trigger a reaction. What I should have done is apologize for the mistake—and take the temperature down a notch. Instead, I fought fire with fire. I confronted him.

As I mentioned earlier, it's not about the chicken. The passenger felt mistreated. Undervalued. He was upset because 1) his meal was burned and 2) it seemed like I didn't really care. I was somewhat sympathetic, but not enough for him. He needed to have his hand held just a little longer.

He needed to feel appreciated.

Like most businesses, airlines don't spend the money to train employees in customer service when it comes to handling moods. It's not viewed as relative to the airlines. But it *is* relative when defective communication impacts customer service.

The first step when it comes to recognizing moods is simple awareness. Let's say you're about to launch a new product. Ninety percent of your workforce is excited about the launch and ready to pour their energies into making this next chapter in the company's history a success.

But a small group in the sales department thinks you're working them too hard already—and this new launch is only adding to that theory. They can't see the possibilities, only the impact the product will have on them personally.

It's the job of a manager or owner to identify that mood and deal with it before it seeps into other departments. To that end, it's vital to understand this basic premise: One size doesn't fit all. Different people require different handling.

Mr. Jones, for example, is coming to work with a mood of deep resentment for reasons unknown. And it's affecting the other salespeople on the team that's down on the new product. Complicating matters is the fact that Mr. Jones for years has been one of the company's top salesmen.

In this case, it's worth exploring the reasons behind Mr. Jones' problem mood. Perhaps, with one-on-one coaching, the issue can be addressed. If the person is open to change and aware that his or her mood is rubbing off on the other employees, there is hope.

On the other hand, employers can't double as therapists. At the end of the day, you're running a business. If the person with the black cloud is dealing with personal issues that fall beyond the scope of team-building exercises or personal coaching, you may have no choice. You don't want clients assessing your company based on the mood of a single person. Sometimes, for the sake of the company, upper management needs to cut the cord, cut their losses, and move on.

The customer isn't the only one who needs to feel appreciated. Reversing the trickle-down flow is no small task for a company whose employees are fueled by resentment. But what too many businesses fail to realize is that it doesn't take a wildly creative gesture to demonstrate appreciation. Simple acknowledgements, even amid economic struggles, can turn the tide and positively impact customer relations. Validate employees. Make them feel heard. Best of all, for those watching the bottom line: It doesn't cost a dime.

After nearly three decades as a flight attendant, I no longer need the validation that maybe I did earlier in my career. But I can see how missed opportunities by management can cause morale issues among the rank and file.

Take the letters we receive from passengers. No one calls you into the office when you receive positive accolades—like the hundreds of notes I've received that are sprinkled throughout this book. Those letters show up in your mailbox.

But one bad letter arrives... and all hell breaks loose.

I've had two such letters in my career. One involved a woman who accused me of not letting her use the first-class bathroom. Because of that, she wet her pants, or so she claimed. Not true.

The second involved a man who took my bags out of the last row of seats, where the flight staff places their belongings, so he could sit next to his wife in that row. When I confronted him, nicely, he became very confrontational. I explained that there were plenty of seats for both of them, but this back row was for the flight crew. There were 50 available seats on this flight. He wrote to my supervisor that I forced him to move (not true) and that there were no seats available (not true). Anyway, each time, I was called to the office. You sit down with the supervisor, read the letter together and discuss it. And it stays in your file as a bad mark.

Think about that. Good letters go to your mailbox. Bad letters, and you're called to the office. It's like you're back in grade school. Without realizing it, this protocol has impacted the mood of the employee. He or she now associates that supervisor, primarily, with something negative.

That's not to say the supervisor shouldn't address personnel problems and customer complaints. But think about what it would mean to the employee if the supervisor called him or her into the office—and read three positive letters.

Suddenly, that person feels appreciated for working at the company—and, most likely, is much less resentful.

It's a simple investment—with a potential for significant returns. This is hardly the only way to change negative, damaging moods. But it's definitely a good start.

I wanted to take a moment to comment on the excellent customer service I received from Becky as well as the entire business class cabin crew on May 24 flight 231 from Miami to LAX I had the distinct pleasure of their services on the five-hour flight. They were both friendly and attentive to all the cabin's needs. Not only did they take care of every request for the passengers in their care, they did it with a smile and friendly demeanor that I have never experienced before in any setting, not just in the airline service. During the flight we were able to laugh and enjoy some brief discussion. I am at a loss for words to really capture the experience. I could only describe it is if we had entered their homes as welcomed guests, not simply as customers they had to serve. I assure you that their customer service will stand out in my mind for a long time to come. In the 15 hours since my flight has landed, I think I've told at least 10 people about my positive experience with this crew. My many thanks for their wonderful service I would love to have them is the crew on all my flights. Regards,

[Name Withheld]

3: LEAVE YOUR BAGGAGE BEHIND

Passenger: *"Do you think my bag will arrive?"*

Flight Attendant: *"Nope. Probably Not. More importantly, would you like something to drink?"*

It was one of those days. I was fried, and in no mood to deal with anyone's crap.

Over the prior weeks, my flight schedule had included a series of international trips. Now, we were on a Boeing 757 going from Miami to St. Thomas, part of the U.S. Virgin Islands. This popular paradise in the middle of the Caribbean Sea is a major destination for second homeowners, vacationers and honeymooners.

In other words, the liquor cart on this flight would be in high demand.

Great. Long distance traveling, in and of itself, can be draining. But flight attendants not only have to deal with the physical tolls that such travel can exact, they also have to work. We're in the same enclosed tube as you, but we're dealing with a full menu of cultures, personalities and moods—and, oh yes, the constant threat of security issues. Throw in the very real possibility of a highly liquored-up crowd (more than 160 passengers on this particular flight), and it doesn't shape up to be a very good day.

I'd been in the business long enough by then to understand that working in customer service requires patience, compassion and sincerity. I had none of that. I missed my bed. I missed my sofa. I missed my television. I missed my dog. I was running on empty.

There were only two of us working the main cabin. Beverage service had yet to start. We were still sitting in our jump seats. A man sitting in the rear of the plane, about four rows from where we were sitting, suddenly walks up, taps me on the shoulder and politely asks if he could order two cocktails, one for him, one for his wife.

The galley flight attendant and I—almost in unison—replied, quite curtly, "We will be with you shortly!"

When the passenger walked away, my co-worker and I started to complain about impatient passengers. We even joked in front of other passengers that this guy must have some kind of drinking problem. Flight attendants and nurses have this in common: We too often talk as if patients/passengers can't hear a thing we're saying. In this case, the last six rows of the main cabin heard our rant.

A feeling of shame came over me. It's not in my nature to be mean-spirited. I knew I had gotten enmeshed in an impromptu bitch session, and I had acted in a way that didn't fit with my moral values. I now felt worse than I did before the flight started!

Later, as we started our beverage service, I could see that the man who tapped me on the shoulder was negatively affected by our less-than-hospitable response to his request. As we passed that row, I finally placed the two cocktails on his wife's tray table. We exchanged glances.

As we were cleaning up prior to landing, I had to maneuver around the galley and aisle to make room for passengers who were going to the lavatory. The man that I had offended was waiting his turn. We struck up a conversation. It turned out that he was going to St. Thomas for the last time to prepare his boat for sale, which he kept in a marina there. The man had been diagnosed with Stage IV prostate cancer. His wife, a breast cancer survivor, had suffered a recurrence of her disease. Her cancer was also Stage IV. As he shared this story, I felt like I had been punched in the stomach. It took everything I had not to break down in front of him. I couldn't have been more ashamed.

I had missed an opportunity, not only as a customer service representative, but as a human being. I could have made this couple's flight something to remember.

Maybe I did ... for all the wrong reasons.

I'm a damn good flight attendant. Sure, on some trips, it takes every bit of strength I have to keep my mean inner-bitch from making an appearance. But I do it because, at the end of the day, I care about my passengers. Otherwise, I wouldn't have lasted thirty years in this industry.

But what I learned that afternoon enroute to St. Thomas was that I can't care about them 99 percent of the time. I can't take a day for myself and write it off to exhaustion or a bad chicken quesadilla at an airport food court. As a cus-tomer-service representative, my clients—the passengers—deserve my "A game" every flight.

They didn't pay to hear me whine or listen to me judge other passengers. I'd let my mood, my selfish behavior, lower the professional bar. In the process, I'd blown a chance to make a difference.

In basketball parlance, I'd shot a customer-service air ball. Worse still, the points were available to me—if only I had ditched that attitude back in the airport parking lot.

But that wasn't the only lesson I took from my St. Thomas disaster.

Standards have come down so much in the airline industry that customers already expect the worst. They expect delays. They expect long security lines. They expect just pretzels and peanuts. In other words, they expect very little.

As a customer-service rep working amid such low expectations, think how easy it is to change the story and make an impact. Now, consider your own business. Maybe the expectations are far greater, given your company's reputation.

Either way, the same opportunity exists—and often with the simplest of gestures. A stranger may not accept that piece of gum you've had in your pocket all flight. But they'll accept an act of kindness.

Think how easy that gesture is—and how little that costs.

When it comes to air travel, people have been mistreated for so long since 9/11 that when a flight attendant shows them kindness, they recognize it right away. I've received more notes from passengers praising my customer-service approach in the past few years than my previous two decades combined. Have I really improved that much as a flight attendant the past few years?

Or are expectations so diminished that simply doing my job—and doing it well—can make a difference in the customer experience? These days, all I have to do is smile at the passengers, and they are happy. They want to feel welcomed. A kind smile goes a long way. Either way, the opportunity is there. Take advantage of it. The payoff, both personally and professionally, is huge.

Not long ago, I was on a flight from Denver to Miami. We diverted to Dallas because the plane needed more fuel. That stop was going to cause a passenger to miss an international flight out of Miami.

After talking to him, I discovered that this man's father was extremely ill and in the hospital. The son was flying overseas to be at his father's side, probably for the final time. I immediately started making calls. It turned out there was a flight from Dallas to that international destination. But, due to regulations, we couldn't make it happen. Instead, we contacted the connecting flight out of Miami, explained the situation, and asked them to wait just 15 minutes for our passenger. The connecting airline agreed. In the meantime, we seated the man in first class for the trip to Miami.

We could have told the man, "Sorry, we're going to be late," and left it at that. We could have made one courtesy call to the connecting flight without pressing the issue. But I listened to his concerns, and I went that extra mile. It cost me nothing to have compassion in my heart for this man.

I was a customer-service person who cared that he wanted to see his dying father. And I found a solution to help him. It's that easy to make a difference.

It's equally easy to turn that same situation into a customer-service nightmare. I've seen flight attendants in similar situations turn a deaf ear to requests—like I did with the St. Thomas passenger with Stage IV cancer.

I can't change the clock if we're running late. But I can be accommodating. I can give you as much information as possible. I can give you a beverage. Mostly, I can validate your feelings.

As a flight attendant, I have a decision. I can throw gasoline on the fire with behavior that alienates the passenger. Or I can understand that there might be reasons beyond the obvious why a person is upset. I can listen. And I can try to diffuse the situation. That is true customer service.

I work first class a lot. And lately I find that almost instinctively I'll place my hand on the shoulder or arm of a passenger when talking to them.

I think I do that because I recognize that people need it. There's a desire for that small slice of affirmation. I'll put my hand on their forearm and ask, "What can I get you to drink?" That simple gesture changes the mood. It warms the cabin. They see that I'm a nice flight attendant. It tells them, "I'm not here to hurt you, I know you've had tough experiences before. I'm here to help."

Passengers expect service problems on plane trips. But I can alter that perception, and so can you in your business, with the simplest of acts. Change the mood, and watch how quickly you enhance the customer-service experience.

May 25, 1990

I took your airline by April '89. But it was no good service. But, this year your all crew is very very nice because every crew is kind and smile, look like they are happy. That is make me happy too. I would like to say about this. You are much nicer than last year. Thanks.

4: WHY JUMP SEAT THERAPY IS NOT THE CURE

Dallas flight attendant to Chicago flight attendant, in a syrupy-sweet Southern drawl: *"Love your hair, hate your guts."*

I can tell you from experience that flights—both long and short—are often filled with all kinds of hot air. Sadly, much of it is coming from the crew.

As the old airline joke goes, there are three ways to communicate: Telephone.

Tell a friend.

Tell a flight attendant.

It's true. Flight attendants love to gossip. And passengers feed into it because we're warm, fuzzy and extroverted. So, they share their life stories with us. We're like a bartender...at thirty-thousand feet. We call it jump-seat therapy.

The problem is that, too often, flight attendants don't know when to stop flapping their own wings. They walk to the back galley and crow about how the person in seat 11C shared a shocking story or a personal detail. From there, one flight crew passes it on to the next crew.

It's like playing telephone as a kid. Except that kids probably are still better at it than flight attendants.

A few years ago, I accidentally fell into a pool during a stopover in Barbados. I bruised three ribs and was sore the next morning, but it felt like one of those injuries that would heal by the end of the week. The return flight was uneventful.

The next day, I was working the main cabin on a flight to San Salvador. While attempting to adjust a bag in the overhead compartment, I lifted and extended my arm. Something happened. The pain in my rib area was excruciating. We landed in San Salvador, and I started having breathing spasms. I went to the hospital there, and sure enough one of my bruised ribs had cracked.

On a flight several months later, one of the attendants said, "Did you hear about our attendant who broke her rib lifting a passenger's bag?" she said. "A passenger asked her to remove it from the overhead bin for him, and the weight of the bag snapped her rib. This is exactly why we shouldn't touch those bags. We get hurt."

I'd been part of the gossip train. I never lifted the bag nor did a passenger ask me to remove it for him. Just elevating my arm broke my previously injured rib. Still, it made for a good story—and it gave the flight attendants another reason to stop helping passengers.

Gossip is one of the quickest ways to create a negative, damaging mood in the workplace. And yet companies rarely address office prattle—even when perception starts to become reality.

For years, rumors flew about one flight attendant. She was a walking, talking nightmare. She had a combative attitude. She treated passengers dismissively. She was mean to co-workers. She was lazy and pawned her work off on other flight attendants. And she rarely reported to work on time.

It made me wonder why someone like this even had a job with the airline. But since I had never met her, I only had stories from my co-workers to go on. So, I bought into the legend of the company's annual "Worst Flight Attendant of the Year" honoree.

That is, until the week I saw that she was on my flight team. I thought about how I was walking into this situation with a preconceived notion, a dismal one at that. And it bothered me. The night before our shift, I decided to wipe the slate clean and give her the chance that she deserved.

The next morning, this "nightmare" employee checked in a full hour earlier than her scheduled start time. She greeted me with a hug and said she had heard so many wonderful things about me as a purser. She couldn't have been more attentive to all the passengers and more pleasant, kind, and professional to the rest of the crew. We had a wonderful flight together.

I'll never know how or why stories about this woman became gospel among other flight attendants. But I'm glad I went into our initial encounter with an open mind.

There may be truth to some rumors, but unless you have first-hand knowledge, isn't it worth giving someone the benefit of the doubt? Even if the stories are true, people do change. It happens all the time. Are you open to that possibility? Or do you have a person permanently boxed in? If so, they'll never change—at least in your mind.

Gossip breeds discontent, resentment, and mistrust in the workplace. If the water-cooler gang will talk about Jerry in accounting, it's a safe bet that they're also talking about you.

I remember overhearing a conversation that the other flight attendants were having about my shoes. I wasn't wearing regulation footwear that day, and the other attendants were talking about it.

Really? My shoes? I interrupted their gossip session and confronted the person leading the charge. I asked her point blank if she had a problem with my wardrobe. "Oh no, I wasn't saying anything." Baloney!

It's ten minutes until takeoff, and there are passengers to assist. But now I'm annoyed. Plus, I'm feeling bullied and frustrated.

This is how quickly gossip can divide the room and alter moods. Instead of worrying about my job, I was thinking about being judged by these catty women wearing regulation shoes.

Managers and CEOs can't put an end to gossip. But they can recognize its impact—and create a company culture that discourages hearsay and mean-spirited small talk, instead of just ignoring it.

Here are just a few reasons why it's worth the effort.

• Gossip causes revenue loss. If you're running your mouth about Sandra, the new salesperson, you're being counterproductive.

• Gossip causes a toxic work environment. It can lead to tensions between employees—or between employees and management. If based on nothing but falsehoods, it also can create reputations that people don't deserve.

• Gossip skews perception. A company may have no intention of cutting staff, but unless upper management addresses a rumor to that effect, workers will think the worst.

• Gossip leads to branding. Would clients rather do business with the company that proudly touts its positives? Or the company that disses the competition at every opportunity? Gossip is not in alignment with integrity—and clients want to do business with the company that shows integrity.

If you're a company owner, put your foot down. There's no place for gossip. It doesn't empower. It demeans the people involved. Acknowledge that you understand it happens. And then try to create an atmosphere where the talk is empowering, not self-sabotaging.

5: DON'T JUDGE THE IN-FLIGHT MAGAZINE BY ITS COVER

"What about when you leave the plane and they've got [the flight attendants] propped by the front door in that complete android catatonic stupor where they look like the Yul Brynner robot from 'Westworld' … 'Bye. Bye. Bye. Bye.' It's like your stockbroker on Thorazine." — Comedian Dennis Miller

Let's be clear about Mr. Miller's observation: In the same way that passengers stereotype those of us who fly the friendly skies for a living, flight attendants also have been known to pass judgment on the man in seat 12B. Or the woman in seat 24A. Or that stand-up comedian sitting in first class.

We sometimes do it from the minute people walk through the cabin doors. Look at the killer heels on that gal. Look at the nightmarish toupee on that guy. Look at Grandma's outfit—did she get that at the flea market? When hundreds upon hundreds of travelers file past you on a given day, it's human nature to make an assessment or two.

After all, being judgmental is almost a default setting—and airports are the perfect place to people-watch. No harm, no foul. Right? But is that really the best way to do business? Or is it a recipe for potential disaster?

It's hard to explain just how nerve-racking it was to go to work as a flight attendant in the months after 9/11. Each time we went to our "office," we were reminded of terrorism. There was no escaping the climate of fear—not to mention the air of suspicion.

Once, on a flight from Miami to Paris two months after the attacks, the alarm went off in a bathroom. Those things don't go off very easily; you can sneak a cigarette in that closet-like space without sounding the alarm. But sure enough, something was burning in this bathroom. You could smell it from several rows away. My first thought was that whoever it was had started a fire.

We quickly shifted into emergency mode. There was no sign of a fire, but we still smelled the strange odor. We had no choice but to treat it as a threat. An air marshal quickly moved to the back of the plane and investigated.

It turned out to be an 18-year-old junkie. He was freebasing cocaine.

I remember checking into the hotel in Paris and nearly dropping to my knees the minute I opened the door to my room. The adrenaline from the initial fear had overwhelmed my system; I was sick the entire layover. Sick from fear.

Not long after that incident, I was the purser on a flight from Miami to New York. One of the flight attendants came rushing up to me with a panicked look on her face.

"We have terrorists on the flight," she said.

I told her to take a breath and calm down. Then I asked, How do you know?"

"They all seem to be from the Middle East," she responded. "They boarded separately, but then they started switching seats. It's clear they know one another. Plus, they're doing these strange word puzzles in Arabic. And they're staring at the passengers. Staring at the flight attendants. It's all too suspicious."

By the time she finished the story, I was freaking out. I went back and made my own assessment of the situation, even though by then my mind was already made up. I had a horrible feeling that we were never going to make it to New York.

I didn't feel safe, and that fear once again was making me physically ill.

I went to the cockpit and explained the situation to the pilots. The pilot decided to return to the gate. The pilot made an announcement to the passengers and soon, air marshals were on the plane. The marshals ordered 11 passengers off of the flight. The suspicious passengers quietly picked up their carry-on bags and said nothing. Not a peep.

We resumed the flight and safely landed in New York. As the passengers were leaving the plane, my cell phone rang. It was my supervisor. He wanted to know why I had removed an entire El Al Airlines flight crew from the plane.

El Al is the national airline of Israel.

In my role as a customer-service representative, I had made a snap judgment. And it cost me.

The passengers were moving around, they were doing puzzles in a strange language—but just because you write in Arabic it doesn't make you a terrorist. I never asked a single question or even attempted to make small talk. It probably would have come out that they were from El Al, which I then could have easily verified before takeoff.

I jumped to a conclusion. And it couldn't have been more wrong.

Before you rush to judgment in a customer-service situation, get your facts straight. The judgments I made were based on my belief system—anyone who jumps from seat to seat is suspicious. Anyone who writes in Arabic is trouble. We were flying to New York. I connected all this to terrorism.

But seeing isn't necessarily believing when it comes to customer service. There has to be room for interpretation.

Why? Because you don't know the first thing about the customer until you begin a conversation. You don't know where they're from or how they were raised.

What inspires them. What frightens them. If they believe in God. If they believe their wife is cheating. If their shoes are causing blisters. If their dog just died.

You don't know a single thing until you ask.

Flight attendants are required by the FAA to approach customers in emergency rows and ask them if they understand the responsibilities that come with sitting in that row. You have to be able to speak English to sit in an emergency row.

On one flight, my co-worker approached a woman of Asian descent. In a loud, borderline demeaning voice, the flight attendant looked directly at the woman and, with a purposely staggered tempo, said, "You ... need ... to be able ... to speak ... English ... to sit ... here."

It turned out the woman was the vice president of an American company. She was Korean but raised in the United States. She didn't speak a word of Korean.

One quick assessment, based on how the woman looked, had caused a major problem. This is a multicultural world. If you do not recognize cultural differences, it's going to be difficult to sustain a business.

What happens when you deal with a person from a completely different culture? Do you let those differences upset you? Do you become annoyed and agitated? Or can you dial down the judgment long enough to understand that every picture tells a story, That is, if you take the time to dig below the surface.

Example: Countless times over the years, I've seen young Haitian girls boarding flights in prom dresses. Do you know why? Humanitarian organizations working with im-poverished Haitians in South Florida will give these girls prom dresses so they have something other than their worn, tattered clothing to wear on the flight.

Who am I to judge that?

We can do much harm when we take people at face value. But we do it anyway. To friends. To family. And, all too often, to complete strangers.

We were flying from Miami to Spain, a good eight-hour trip, on a huge 767. One of my flight attendants pulled me aside before takeoff and said there was a passenger in the back who needed to be removed.

"We already removed her once, three days ago, and she's back on again," the flight attendant reported, "We're not taking her; she's too ill to travel."

Another flight attendant came up and said the same thing. "This passenger shouldn't be flying. She's going to die in mid-flight. I'm not dealing with this."

I told them, "I can't remove a passenger based on your last experience with her if you don't have a good reason now."

The proof, they said, was in the visual evidence. It was true she looked quite ill. But there was a good reason. She had recently suffered a stroke. According to airline standards, those passengers clearly incapable of taking care of themselves do need a travel companion. Three days earlier, she didn't have a caretaker. This time, she did.

It was her husband. Both he and his wife were in their 70s. He was tending to her just fine. And I saw no reason to remove them. I insisted that we keep her on the flight, and my supervisor agreed with me. The flight attendants spent the entire eight hours complaining about this woman.

After the plane landed, the other passengers filed out one by one down the two aisles, leaving just the man and his wife. The husband was struggling to gather their belongings and assist his wife. Across the aisle, the still-angered flight attendants did absolutely nothing to help. They stood there and watched.

I went up to the couple, helped them collect their things and assisted her into her wheelchair. The woman muttered something that I couldn't quite understand. I leaned down, and she whispered, "Thank you for being so kind to me."

I watched the husband wheel his wife up the ramp, and then I buried my head in my hands and began to cry.

The woman knew what the flight attendants had done to her the previous flight. She also knew that they were complaining about her this time. I couldn't believe my co-workers could be so cruel to another human being. It was the most shameful incident I've ever been involved with.

"Sir, turn your cell phone off," I said.

If only I had a nickel for every time I made that request—only to have it ignored. When I'm tired, I notice that defiance of the "cell phone rule" quickly sets me off.

Once, I asked an older gentleman to turn off his cell phone. He pretended to turn it off, or so I thought, by putting it on stand-by mode. In front of everyone, I said,

"You're kidding, right? Do you think I'm stupid?" I kind of went off on him.

His son leaned across the aisle and said, "Dad, let me have your phone." And he turned it off.

"You didn't have to be so mean about it," the son said to me.

He was right. I didn't have to be so mean. Later in the flight, I went back and apologized to the son.

"My father really doesn't understand how to turn the phone off," he said. "He hits a few buttons, but it never shuts off."

"My father doesn't know how to turn his phone off either," I said. "I'm so sorry."

I had a belief that this man thought I was a dumb stewardess who didn't know anything; he was disrespecting me. The truth is that I didn't feel good about myself in that moment.

I didn't mean to be a bitch, but I was. I was tired and frustrated. The difference, in this case, is that I cleaned up my mess. I went back and apologized. Most people don't.

There's no power in making snap judgments. Yes, we have to make assessments at times, but they should be assessments grounded in truth. The quicker employees understand and practice that sentiment, the stronger your company's customer-service reputation will become.

A few years ago, an overweight woman boarded the plane. You could see the fear in her eyes. Soon, I learned why. It was her very first flight. But something else wasn't right. Her possessions were all in a garbage bag. She didn't look well enough to travel—and she overlapped into another seat.

Once again, there was talk of removing her. But it became my mission to see that didn't happen. I wasn't stranding this passenger. My heart went out to her.

Later in the flight, I started making small talk with her. In turns out, she had just been released from prison after twenty years behind bars. I didn't ask why.

She was sick, very sick. She was going home to spend her final weeks with her family. When she talked about her family, her eyes lit up. She was so happy to be going home.

I gave her as much attention as possible. I wanted her first and last flight to be above and beyond. That wasn't the place to pass judgment. But it was the time to take good care of a customer.

The purpose of this letter is to thank you for the services I received from a flight attendant based in Raleigh Durham, Miss Becky Silvera. I have recently begun to fly on a frequent basis and I've had the occasion to experience several levels of customer service. It is in my opinion that Ms. Silvera exemplifies that service at its best. On Sunday, 14 August 1988 I traveled from DFW to RDU. It was 107° outside and the aircraft seemed uncomfortably warm even after we were airborne for some time. From my vantage point it was evident that Miss Silvera took every opportunity to make a cramped, hot, extremely crowded if not full flight more pleasant. She handled her duties calmly, expeditiously and with the friendly attitude even when some of her passengers were ill mannered and impatient. I feel that repeat business is critical to success in the fiercely competitive airline industry as with any service related enterprise. I look forward to flying with your airline again and possibly being served by Ms. Silvera. Please pass my compliments on to her.

Thank you again,
Sincerely,

[Name Withheld]

6: HOW TO DEAL WITH DELAYS

Passenger: *"Every time I fly this airline I'm delayed."*
Flight attendant: *"Oh! Then it must be you."*

 Baggage handlers have a thankless job. In some ways, they're a lot like football referees. People only notice them when they make mistakes—or when they get run over. These days baggage handlers all wear vests with reflective material so that they're easily seen in the dark. But back in the day that wasn't always the case. On occasion, we'd have delays because a baggage handler was in the wrong place at the wrong time.

One night, the plane had pulled out of the gate while the baggage handler was still in the area. Maybe he was in the pilot's blind spot, who knows? The plane came to a screeching halt, the baggage handler escaped without being pinned beneath a 737 and the area was cleared. A mechanic made sure nothing had happened to the landing gear when the pilot slammed on the brakes.

As the mechanic began troubleshooting the area, his jacket got stuck in a piece of equipment, and the plane couldn't start.

Believe me, stranger things have happened during my three decades as a flight attendant. But, to the passenger, the incident contributed to the public's negative image of the airline industry.

We broke a commitment. We told you we were going to leave in five minutes, but it ended up being five hours.

In business, the clock never stops ticking. So, what do you do when time isn't on your side? When, through no fault of your own, a delay breaks the covenant of trust you're trying to build with your customer?

As I've discovered all too often, the key is to make each second count.

People think the airlines lie all the time. They think they lie about fares. About baggage. About running out of blankets. But mostly they think we lie about delays.

It's a beautiful day outside. Not a cloud in the sky. So how can the flight from Atlanta to Tampa possibly be late by 40 minutes? And how am I now supposed to make my connecting flight in Houston when I'll have five minutes to race across George Bush Intercontinental Airport?

Passengers don't understand why the plane was delayed—and honestly they don't care. They just know it's unacceptable.

Anyone in business recognizes this situation. Let's say a package didn't arrive as promised. Timing gone awry.

No matter the cause, you have to deal with it.

So how do you respond?

You could say, "I'm not sure what happened, but we'll get it to you next week."

Or this: "I agree with you. This is a breakdown. We made a mistake."

As a customer-service agent, it's not up to me to teach you morals and standards on how to be a better person in that situation. The customer has every right to be mad. It's about how I can address your complaints to your satisfaction.

I like to start with a little accountability. Admit the mistake. Confession can be good for the soul in this case.

From there, it's all about listening.

That's it. You can't imagine how many situations are diffused that way. I can't change the clock if we're running late. I can't go back in time and tuck in the mechanic's sleeve so that it doesn't get caught in the landing gear. But I can be accommodating. I can give you as much information as possible. I can give you a beverage.

Mostly, I can validate your feelings. You're ticked; I get it. But I'm not going to add to the cabin pressure by confronting you.

Passengers, believe it or not, aren't the only ones pulling out their hair when a flight is delayed. The airline industry works on a strict clock. One misstep during the day can create a domino effect.

There's a term in the industry called the "kickoff flight." Some planes fly 24 hours straight. "Kickoff flight" refers to a plane that has been at rest during the night. It's the first plane out that morning, and it's the most crucial flight of the day because of the potential trickle-down effect.

Let's say something happens prior to takeoff creating an unwanted situation that keeps the kickoff flight grounded for an hour. Now, connections all over the country are impacted. The snowball is rolling.

By mid-afternoon, you could be talking about hundreds of missed connections. By night's end, you could be talking about ticket refunds. Free tickets, depending on the situation. Passengers having to spend the night at an airport hotel.

It's said that one canceled flight in Madrid can cause a three-day disruption on a European route, sometimes longer. I've heard of backlogs that extend to three months, all because of one canceled flight.

Being late is a financial sinkhole for the airline industry. It opens up the potential for lost revenue, lost goodwill, and lost customers. Time, in this case, really is money.

But not all delays hit your company in the checkbook. Sometimes, being late is all about perception and a little something called respect.

John is one of your company's most talented employees. But he's always late to work. Tuesday, he was supposed to be here at 8. He showed up at 8:15. Wednesday, we had a lunchtime meeting slated for 11:30. He showed up at 11:40.

In the same way that passengers lose their trust when an airline is late, an employer loses his trust in an employee that can't make a scheduled time to save his life. The employer also feels slighted. Tardiness is a lack of commitment; the employee doesn't care enough about the company to show up on time. And that speaks to integrity.

So, what do you do as an employer?

For starters, ground your assessment in fact. And then communicate to that person why it's important to you that he or she shows up on time. Too often, parents and bosses admonish without explanation. Give them an opportunity to change, but communicate why being prompt is a reflection on the entire company. If you commit to be there at eight, show up at eight– or earlier.

It's a simple premise, but it can speak volumes about your attention to detail. John is untrustworthy because he's always late to business meetings, thus your company is untrustworthy.

Being late can overwhelm your business. If you let John skate on the tardiness issue, it's eventually going to trickle down into customer service. And, you're showing contempt for your clients, the foundation on which your business is built.

Harvard once did a study that suggested it takes seven or eight times for an action to be repeated before someone will make a new assessment on that person. The airline suffering from consistent delays must do a series of things to make up for this over a set period of time to rebuild trust and change the culture of a company.

Success is in the details, and in this case, time is of the essence. Don't let someone like John create an unnecessary negative storyline that is embarrassing to your company.

I have flown many times in my life and enjoy travel. go to Las Vegas once or twice a year I'm a registered nurse now for 34 years. Want to tell you about a few people you have working for you. They deserve a lot of praise and reward and recognition for all they had to endure well trying to get to flight 612 well trying to get flight 612 off the ground. The first delay was a box not working— supposed to be a 15-minute delay. Next, they had to fly one in from California, the box. The pilot started the engine and it wouldn't work. We all got off again into the waiting area and by this time of the passengers, a large number we're really upset. We sat around and talked about it, and with all of their screaming and yelling, it sure was not the fault of the desk or ship crew that the plane wasn't working. I have been in the people business now for many years and worked with all kinds of individuals, but the pleasant, patient, professional way your staff conducted themselves was above and beyond the call of duty. If I were able to reward them I sure would do so; we were delayed about 8 to 9 hours and I'm sure they were as tired as we. Thank you for listening, and please give these people my very best. I hope I am privileged to travel with them again Sincerely,

[Name Withheld]

7: BENEFITS OF UPRIGHT POSITION

I've never been on a plane that had to park in a cornfield—knock on wood— but I do know when something isn't right on an aircraft. Flight attendants are the eyes and ears of the plane. We can tell when there's an air leak. We know the look on a passenger's face who is struggling with travel anxiety. I've been on so many different planes that I can even smell trouble in air—and not just from the people trying to sneak a smoke in the bathroom.

But even the best training in the world doesn't always prepare flight attendants for heavy turbulence.

I've been on planes that took such dramatic drops that it felt like being on the Tower of Terror at Disney's Hollywood Studios. For those of us working the cabin— and not wearing seatbelts—such rollercoaster rides put us directly in the line of fire.

I've seen several flight attendants bash their heads against overhead bins. I saw one attendant slice her hand open on a wine bottle that exploded. Another suffered three cracked ribs when the service cart rammed into her side. I even watched one co-worker propelled across the galley by heavy turbulence. When she tried to brace for the fall, her index finger became lodged in the countertop grate, slicing the tip of it right off.

Once during a flight on a small plane to the Bahamas, the turbulence was so bad that it felt like the plane was coming apart at the seams. I was a passenger on this flight, but I still was in uniform. I thought we were going down. It was like being inside one of those Bingo ball machines; everything was bouncing up and down. Even the tiniest piece of paper flew out of my pocket. So, I started crying.

I felt like everyone on the plane had turned to look at me. If the flight attendant is crying, it must be trouble. The plane survived the Bingo ball turbulence, but I learned a few valuable lessons that day.

For starters, the uniform means something. Uniforms represent the brand of the company.

One time, a passenger told me I had forgotten his drink. I told him he had not asked me for a drink. He argued that he did. A few seconds later, I found the flight attendant with whom he had placed his order. She was a brunette, and 20 years older than me. I was a blonde

"Well, you all look alike to me," the passenger grumbled.

He only saw the uniform. But that's not my concern. My concern is the connection that a customer makes between the uniform and the company. How I act while serving in that uniform can impact that perception.

Let's say a challenging situation has developed at your office, one that requires an immediate decision. The head of the company isn't around. The general manager is on vacation. The only senior employee available to deal with it is you—and the clock is ticking.

Are you the kind of employee who would seize the opportunity to shine? Or would the moment leave you paralyzed and indecisive?

In business, just as during a turbulent flight, employees must be prepared to think on their feet and make a move.

Long ago, as part of our cart service, flight attendants served coffee out of old-school metal pots. Once, during a bouncy flight, a co-worker lost control of this heavy coffee pot, and it flew right into the lap of an elderly gentleman.

Now what? A pot filled with steaming hot coffee just land-ed in the crotch of a 75-year-old man. Do you run from the situation? Do you make a break for the emergency exit? That's not likely to happen at 35,000 feet. Guess what? Shit happens—and, more often than not, it's out of your con-trol.

So, deal with it. You can't change what just happened. But you can try and win back the business. So stay cool. Be present. Show your face; don't hide and pretend like it didn't happen. Don't make excuses. And do whatever it takes to let the passenger/customer know that you care.

By being decisive, managing the situation and keeping the customer front and center, you can do more than just sal-vage a potential disaster. You also can demonstrate, to any-one watching, that yours is a lead worth following.

I can't tell you how many times I've seen co-workers crumble in the face of adversity. Over the years, I've dealt with flight attendants who wanted to bail on their duties because they "partied too hard" the night before. More than once, I've had to play amateur psychologist because a flight attendant was going through a breakup that was af-fecting her work.

One time, a co-worker nearly threw a tantrum because she forgot her corkscrew—and she had eight first-class passengers waiting for wine. I walked up to her, reached for a butter knife ... and showed her how to push the cork through the bottle so she could pour.

Work the problem. Keep the customer happy.

It's sounds so simple on paper, but it's amazing how often the slightest curve in the road can derail an employee…and, sometimes, an entire company.

I remember being on a 727 during the final leg of a cross-country flight, with only a handful of passengers—the majority of them in first class, which was my territory that night. It was dinnertime, and I was heating meals for about twelve people. As I went to plate the first dinner, I realized that we had a serious problem.

There were no plates. None in the front galley. Nothing in the storage area. None in the back galley.

It's times like this that you have to be resourceful. I took the covers off the cooking containers, plated the meals neatly on the cardboard, and explained to first class what had happened. The passengers loved it—mostly because, plates or not, they still received their food. Instead of saying, "Sorry, no dinner tonight," I found a way to serve them.

The lesson, whether you're serving first class or dealing with a situation at your place of business, is simple: Don't give up. Weigh all the possibilities instead throwing in the towel. You might just solve the problem and solidify a business relationship all in one shot.

Planes break down. We're talking about large, complicated pieces of machinery with all kinds of moving parts. Some of the best mechanics in the world earn their keep by poring over each part of the plane to ensure passenger safety.

So why do passengers get so upset when a mechanical malfunction causes a delay?

It changes their day. They depend on the airline to get them to their destination on time. Suddenly, that promise has been broken. Passengers need to reschedule meetings, vacation arrivals, start times for family gatherings, you name it. One minor fix, let's say an engine problem that requires no more than a 30-minute delay, can cause a chain reaction that impacts passengers, friends, family and businesses all over the world.

From a business standpoint, there's something worth noting about the way passengers deal with delays. I see some people handle it without an issue. They make the call, change the business meeting, change the time on their rental car, and everything is right with the world.

Other people lose it. This one glitch throws their life into chaos. They complain to the airline reps, they make calls to family and friends and gripe so loud that people three terminals away can hear. They play the victim card and try to snag free flights.

On one painfully memorable occasion, a female passenger physically assaulted the female gate agent from our airline due to a flight delay. And not just a slap or two. This woman literally beat and kicked our gate agent—all while a circle of people just stood around watching. It took a passenger walking to another flight to look over, see what was happening, and help. By the way, who just stands there and does nothing when someone is getting pummeled?

You want people to follow your lead? React to the person who needs help! Different people deal with stress in different ways. As a leader, you can't allow stress to elevate a workable situation into complete chaos.

There always will be breakdowns in daily life. How you handle it says a lot about how you are as a communicator and who you are as a person. If you live in a state of anger, how can you resolve problems?

From an attitude standpoint, compassion goes a long way. So, does staying calm and professional, even in the face of someone doing neither.

It also helps to give people the tools to solve their problem. I can't tell you how many times I've loaned my cell phone to people whose phones have died, especially in other countries. Not every solution is steeped in creativity and genius. Simple acts of kindness can go a long way toward changing people's moods and winning the day forever.

8: YOU MAY EXPERIENCE TUR-BULENCE

A passenger exclaimed, *"Great service! And it doesn't hurt that you have nice legs too!"*

"Extra hands assure extra luxuries." —1959 ad for Delta's Royal Service flights, featuring three "alert stewardesses" instead of just two

National Airlines wasn't the only carrier to objectify and disrespect flight attendants during the Sexy Seventies. But its advertising campaign that ran for the better part of five years, starting in 1971, certainly pushed the notion that sex sells to new heights.

"I'm Jo. Fly me."

"I'm Cheryl. Millions of people flew me last year."

"I'm Laura. I'll fly you nonstop from London to Miami any morning at 10:40. Something else I'll do is help you have fun getting there. With movies. … And lots of personal attention."

By today's standards, and especially through the lens of a post-Weinstein et al world, it's hard to believe such demeaning and chauvinistic ads found their way into newspapers and magazines. But not everyone in those days viewed the campaign with a wink and a nudge.

Feminist groups, led by the National Organization for Women (NOW) (which tried to use legal means to block the ads from running), criticized the "Fly Me" spots as being overtly sexist. Not only did the NOW complaint fall on deaf ears, but National, which was taken over by Pan Am in 1980, saw a roughly 20-percent spike in business early in the campaign.

National certainly wasn't alone in marketing its flight attendants as sex objects—or, better still, marriage material.

United actually ran a campaign that included the pitch, "Every [passenger] gets warmth, friendliness and extra care. And someone may get a wife."

American Airlines, meanwhile, seemed to be running its own dating service. Its advertising contribution introduced us to a woman named Sandy, who's quoted as saying, "I always feel like I'm sort of giving a party." American promised its customers that "we'll keep combing America for girls like Sandy. And as soon as we meet them, we promise to introduce them to you."

Delta bypassed the flight attendant completely and instead appealed to "the guy who's got a girl in every city." Its ad from this era included photos of six different women living in different major markets, among them "Your San Francisco sweetie," "Your New York knockout," and "Your Miami minx." The fine print explained that Delta's fast nonstop flights get your trip off to a flying start, "so you [have] more time—and more money—to fly high with her."

My, how times have changed in the airline industry. Or have they?

Less than a decade ago, an advertisement for a Thai airline sought "beautiful girls with nice personalities" for its flight attendant openings. The ad also noted that only women 25 and under should apply.

In 2012, backlash over newspaper ads from the Irish airline Ryanair that left little to the imagination; think bikini-clad flight attendants and the catch-phrase "red hot fares and crew." This prompted the Advertising Standards Authority to ban the campaign.

It took Qatar Airways (fully government owned) until 2015 to change its archaic policies restricting female cabin crew employees from marrying or becoming pregnant.

All of this should come as a shock, shouldn't it? We've come so far since Jo and Cheryl and Laura told us to fly them, right? Wrong. Four decades later, there are flight attendants who still battle perception problems and, in some cases, outright abuse.

In 2014, the Equal Opportunities Commission (EOC) released a survey it had conducted with the Hong Kong Flight Attendants Alliance. Of the 392 flight attendants (86 percent of them female) who completed the questionnaire, 27 percent acknowledged that they had been sexually harassed while on duty during the prior year.

The harassment encompassed everything from offensive jokes to inappropriate physical contact, including kissing and pinching. Nearly six out of every 10 claims involved actions by customers. The rest of the harassment involved co-workers.

Businesses around the world battle negative stereotypes that may or may not be accurate. This shipping company is too slow. That fast-food chain has the worst fries. This law firm overcharges. That hospital keeps patients waiting too long.

After decades of dealing with the stereotypes that come with being a flight attendant, I'm certain that the most pressing issue isn't always whether businesses are willing to change the narrative.

Sometimes, it's whether they even recognize that the stereotype exists!

Back in the day, I worked with a group of pilots who had this not-so-secret gauge for prospective dates or one-night encounters. They would put their hands straight out, with their two thumbs touching and their two index fingers extended, to form something that recalled a football goalpost. That was the test for these pilots: If a woman's behind was wider than that, they wouldn't hit on her.

What I found ironic about this test is that the pilots' own behinds got bigger and wider with each passing year.

Welcome to my world. I may have missed the "Fly Me" era, but, trust me, I dealt with more than my share of preconceived notions about flight attendants.

The stereotypes went something like this:

Flight attendants have nothing going on upstairs, especially those of us who were any shade of blonde.

We were uneducated, and probably a cheerleader back in high school.

Ours wasn't a "real career."

Being a pilot is a real career. How could we possibly earn enough money to sustain ourselves as flight attendants. Ironically, in my divorce settlement in 1999, I had to pay my husband—a pilot—a substantial portion of my earnings because I made more than he did at that time.

We had a limited shelf life, given that our job was based on our looks.

We were loose…or even slutty.

Our in-flight kindness proved we were loose. One time, a passenger boldly asked me to sleep with him after our plane touched down. I told him I was married. He said so was he. I asked him what possibly made him think I was interested. "Well," he said, "you were awfully nice to me during the flight."

Years later, when I was running my own business, an acquaintance approached me during a networking event with an observation he believed might be of help. He felt that I brought on unwanted advances because of my outgoing personality—and that some people didn't take me seriously in business as a result.

Listen, I have a big personality. And I'm friendly by nature. That doesn't mean I want to sleep with you.

But I digress.

By the time I started as a flight attendant in 1987, the industry, in some ways, already was changing. Thanks to the ruling in a 1981 discrimination lawsuit brought against Southwest Airlines, which wouldn't hire male flight attendants or ticket agents at the time, more men were now asking passengers to return their tray tables to an upright position. (Southwest's contention—and, remember, this was the early '80s—was that beautiful female flight attendants played into the airline's "sexy" image and, thus, was an occupational qualification for the gig; the judge shot that argument down.)

But the more some things changed, the more other aspects of the industry stayed the same.

Pilots still ruled the roost, and flight attendants needed to know their place. In my early days, several pilots I knew wore their "Father Knows Best" hat in the cockpit—and their Hugh Hefner pajamas in the hotel lounge.

These were the pilots who felt flight attendants were there to look good and to serve them. I can't tell you how many times a pilot required his food and drink before anyone else on the plane. The sense of entitlement was nauseating.

It reminded me of this airline manual I once came across, a set of instructions about in-flight protocol that was printed back in the 1950s. It mentioned how the stewardess should be at the pilot's beck and call. The stewardess was even expected to place a dinner napkin over the pilot's shirt, so it wouldn't get stained during dinner. Way beyond nauseating.

But that manual was minor compared to the maintenance log kept on the plane during my early years of flying. The log included an equipment list for the engineer to check before passengers boarded—as well as an impressive selection of centerfold photos that had been cut out of "Playboy," or some other nudie magazine, and taped into the back pages by both the engineers and pilots.

Sometimes, events beyond the business have a way of changing the narrative. The centerfold pages, for example, disappeared from the log book shortly after Anita Hill testified in 1991 that then-Supreme Court nominee Clarence Thomas sexually harassed her. Thomas would be confirmed, but the airline industry seemed to have a sudden revelation around that time: The cockpit should no longer double as a frat house.

But the best businesses don't need a national controversy to right a wrong. They understand exactly what's happening behind the cockpit door. They engage their employees, they ask the right questions, and they pay attention to shifts in the workplace atmosphere. If there's truth in a prevailing negative perception, the best managers are proactive about dealing with it in the moment.

My airline didn't hire new personnel for several years after 9/11; many airlines were forced to lay off employees during that time. When we finally ended the freeze, something had changed—and for the better. The new flight attendant hires had been evaluated on their ability to problem-solve and deliver the best customer service.

Were candidates judged on their looks? To some extent, always. But I also saw people with tattoos being hired. In my early days, that was a deal-breaker. People once considered "overweight" by industry standards (in the old days, you could be fired for being too heavy) were now part of the team—because, really, you don't have to be ultra-skinny to properly pass out bags of pretzels.

Those changes had nothing to do with 9/11. It was more about recognizing and dealing with the final remnants of the "Fly Me" stereotype. For sure, the industry had evolved over the years. But it was time for one last push. In the process, the emphasis on service changed the narrative.

It didn't happen overnight for the airline industry; in fact, it took the better part of a half-century. But in the business world at large, for a more enlightened manager or executive, perhaps it can happen overnight.

Don't wait. Identify the challenges in your business, make the appropriate adjustments—and watch perception, the perception you've always envisioned, become reality.

✈

There was a time in my career when I'd go with the other flight attendants to the hotel bar during an overnight layover, and, inevitably, we'd hang out with the pilots. As I got older, I became part of the crew that the pilots labeled "slam-clickers." These were the women, many of them married, who either left the bar early or who stayed in their rooms all night. Those doors were slammed shut and locked, thus the slam-clicker reference.

I have to say, I loved being a slam-clicker. It was my time to call room service, catch up on TV or read a book. The last few years of my career, I never left the hotel room.

Considering the recently escalated national discussion about sexual harassment, I'm now wondering if slam-clicker didn't have a second meaning—especially for those pilots rejected in the wee hours by having a hotel door slam in their faces.

That said, things can happen after a few drinks in a hotel bar. Pilots and flight attendants hooked up back then, and they still do today. Sometimes, passengers and flight attendants end up together.

And sometimes, pilots and passengers cross the line with flight attendants.

I've been asked several times of late if I was ever sexually harassed during my 30-year career. The answer is no. That's because I wouldn't allow it.

For me, harassment is when you say no, and the person continues to act in an inappropriate manner. If I hear something that rubs me the wrong way, I'm not afraid to speak up. That always has worked for me. I quickly establish ground rules, and I'm blunt about it. "Stop it, or you'll feel the back end of this high heel."

That's not to say someone can't push my buttons. The last time someone said something that really got under my skin, it actually was a female pilot. She called me, "Sweetie." It wasn't the word, it was the tone. She was so condescending, as if being in the same room with a flight attendant was an issue for her. Like I was a dimwit for not going to pilot school.

That's on me. That speaks to my beliefs and my insecurities. She triggered an emotion in me, and I let it get to me. What are my options in that moment? Quit? Pout? Take a swing at her? I could have created chaos in that moment. Instead, I communicated my issue with what she said. I asked the pilot, moving forward, not to address me that way. I shut that behavior down. Just as I shut it down when male pilots overstep their boundaries.

You can't change jobs every time there's a challenge. Deal with an issue in the moment. Don't let it linger. Don't let the bitterness build. That leads to passive aggressive behavior in the future. Or late-night emails that you regret sending the following morning.

I've been called a bitch more than once during my flight attendant career. Honestly, I'm not offended. Nine times out of 10, it's because I'm doing something you don't like. It's because I'm an assertive woman who speaks her mind.

"Oh, she's such a bitch."

No, she's not. She's standing up for what she believes. She's also standing her ground. She's saying, "What you're saying or doing to me is not appropriate."

It's time for more women to be that strong, assertive bitch to get what they want and need.

Or, like me, to be that Sky Bitch.

ABOUT THE AUTHOR

Becky Woodbridge

Whether 30,000 feet in the air or on land, Becky Woodbridge has made a career of helping people get what they want: good service.

She is a recently retired 30-year flight attendant/purser who at the same time owned a highly-rated real estate company in the busy, South Florida residential market.

Most recently, she was event producer/curator for the popular TED talks, TEDxBocaRaton, an independently organized TED event, and Contagious Optimism, attended by more than 5,000 people.

In 2016, Becky founded SkyBitch™ LLC, where she is chief empowerment officer. SkyBitch empowers women to find their "inner bitch" and is devoted to helping women be more powerful, courageous, independent, dignified and successful.

In addition to her strong stance in helping women, Becky educates businesses and individuals on the secrets of superb customer service, company culture, and public identity. Her topics include strategies to improve moods of both employees and clients, and to heal communication breakdowns.

Always an optimist herself, Becky co-authored the books, *Contagious Optimism* and *10 Habits of Truly Optimistic People*. Her next book, *The Making of a SkyBitch: From Doormat to Serial Entrepreneur*, will be released in 2018.

Known as a creative thinker, Becky gives freely of her time. Born in Bangor, Maine, she migrated to South Florida, and was a regional business leader for more than a dozen years. Becky now resides in Durango, Colorado with her daughter EJ, and their dog, Lady Glitter Sparkles.

www.ingramcontent.com/pod-product-compliance
Lightning Source LLC
Chambersburg PA
CBHW050512210326
41521CB00011B/2421